HI AARON — I HOPE
YOU LIKE MY BOOK.
LOVE,

POCO :

Norman Ward

HI! MY NAME IS POCO

A true story by Norman Ward

AuthorHouse™
1663 Liberty Drive,
Suite 200
Bloomington, IN 47403
www.authorhouse.com
Phone: 1-800-839-8640

AuthorHouse™ UK Ltd.
500 Avebury Boulevard
Central Milton
Keynes, MK9 2BE
www.authorhouse.co.uk
Phone: 08001974150

First published by AuthorHouse 10/26/2006

ISBN: 1-4259-7584-4 (sc)

Printed in the United States of America
Bloomington, Indiana

This book is printed on acid-free paper.

Cover design and interior layout by the Legwork Team

Bloomington, IN Milton Keynes, UK

authorHOUSE™

Dedicated to Ellie, my lifelong love,
and, of course, Poco.

Hi! My name is Poco. I'm a Portuguese Water Dog, which is a funny name for me—because I don't like going into the water. Every time my owners, Ellie and Norman, try to carry me into our pool, I paddle quickly to the steps—and get out fast! I'm afraid I'll sink.

Even a piece of chicken won't make me go in there!

This is me with Ellie by my first home.

When I was a puppy, I had an amazing adventure. Instead of going to a new house like most puppies do, I went across the whole country— from New York to California—in a motor home! It was a very small one, so it was very easy to step on me. Ouch!

That's me tied to a tree at a beautiful campsite.

At night we always stayed at a campsite. Ellie and Norman kept me tied to a tree with a long rope because I liked to run off and explore places and do my favorite things; eating everything I see and playing with anything I can reach. What fun I had ripping up Ellie's straw hat, unrolling toilet paper and chewing up maps, shoes and campfire stuff. I don't know why they got so annoyed with me.

Once in California, we visited Ellie and Norman's old friends, Gerry and Jeanne. I had fun there because they didn't know me and left all kinds of interesting things on the floor. They had Indian musical instruments all over the place and I had such a delightful time chewing up a small drum beater. I didn't know what loud voices were until I heard Aunt Jeanne when she found out what I had done! I was tied up outside for the rest of our visit.

We were on the road for one month making lots of friends—who always wanted me tied up. I don't know why. I just liked chewing things to pieces.

By the way, I love people and whenever I meet new ones I jump up on them and give them friendly little love bites. It's my way of showing them that I like them. But they do funny things like saying, "Norman, what's that dog doing now?"

When we finished our cross-country trip, I learned about my new house. I loved it. There was lots of stuff there to chew up. I ate pencils, pens, pills—anything I could find. Little by little, my owners started putting things in high places where I couldn't reach them. Before everything disappeared from my sight, I ruined two radio remote controls, a blood pressure kit, Norman's sneakers and Ellie's earrings.

Here I am in my new home getting what I like the most.

Here I am on the deck with my friend Woody after a snow storm.

Here I am walking my cousin Hudson.

One day Ellie and Norman decided that I should be taken to an obedience school. I don't know why. There was a whole room full of dogs at the school. We all learned to walk close to our owners and always on their left sides. We learned other things, too. I was a good student and loved being with other dogs.

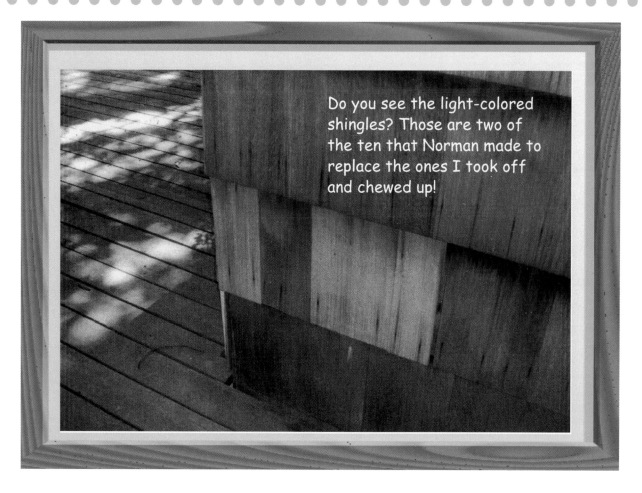

Do you see the light-colored shingles? Those are two of the ten that Norman made to replace the ones I took off and chewed up!

When we got home, I was so happy and proud of myself for doing such a great job at obedience school that I just felt like chomping on something. I don't know why, but Norman was annoyed with me when I ripped ten shingles from the house, and of course, chewed them. Norman spoke to me in a stern way. I was never spoken to in that way before. HE WAS MAD!

After a long time, he replaced all of the missing shingles himself and I decided I'd better not touch them again.

Ellie suggested that more exercise might be good for me, so one day she and Norman took me to an agility class. It was indoors in a large room that was full of really fun things for dogs like me to do. There were curved tunnels to go through, up and down ramps, tires to jump through and poles to go in and out of. I loved those things and did very well. --- Got a lot of cookies too!

When the weather got warmer, the class moved outside and I was also very good at all of the tricks there. There was just one problem: The second they took my leash off, I would run away so I could smell things and look at plants and watch bugs and stuff. I didn't want to go back to the class. After I dashed off to explore like that in the next few sessions, the teacher told Ellie and Norman that she didn't think I belonged in the class anymore. I don't know why. I did all the tricks.

At home, I heard my owners say, "This is the first time anyone in our family has been asked to leave a class."—I think they were crying.

This is what an agility course looks like. Can you count all the things I did?

I just had my first birthday. I heard Norman say, "Hey, Poco is only one. Children hardly can walk at that age. They can barely talk and they have to be fed by adults. Look at all that he can do. He doesn't know the difference between what's bad and good yet, but he's learning. Let's give him time."—Sounded good to me—as I broke the frame of Ellie's glasses and lost one of the lenses.

Little by little, I stopped eating things like electric wires, shoes, toilet paper, clothing, furniture, pottery, my toys, towels, baskets and other things.

When I reached the age of two, I knew that they liked me much more—I still give strangers friendly little love bites because I like everybody.

I'm Poco.

HI! MY NAME IS POCO

Purchase this book from your favorite bookstore, or online from
AuthorHouse.com, Amazon.com, BarnesAndNoble.com, Borders.com

Author Norman Ward has a varied history of teaching music in schools, composing music for orchestra, band and chorus as well as writing magazine articles on diverse topics. This book was triggered by a string of misadventures with the family's first "challenging" dog. Norman lives in Dix Hills, New York with wife Ellie and Poco.

Printed in the United States
65179LVS00001B